**this
strawberry book
belongs to**

This book is for
Christopher
Nicholas
Gillian
and
Johnathan.
My favorite little
bears.

Library of Congress Cataloging in Publication Data

Hefter, Richard.
  One bear, two bear.

  "A strawberry book."
  SUMMARY: Zany bears count the numbers from 1 to 10.
  1. Counting—Juvenile literature. [1. Counting]
I. Title.
QA113.H43   513'.2   80-16544
ISBN 0-07-027825-3

McGraw-Hill Book Company
1221 Avenue of the Americas
New York, N.Y. 10020

one bear
two bears

the strawberry™ number book

by Richard Hefter

a strawberry book™
McGraw-Hill Book Company
New York   St. Louis   San Francisco   Toronto
Hamburg   Mexico

One bear, two bears;
Where are you bears?

Three bears, four bears;
Through the door bears.

Five bears, six bears;
Do some tricks bears.

Seven bears, eight bears;
Watch the skate bears!

Nine bears, ten bears;
Start again bears.

Ten bears running down the road;
One stops off to watch a toad.

Nine bears charging up the hill;
One bear trips and takes a spill.

Eight bears waiting for a bus;
One decides to hide from us.

Seven bears walking, single file;
One bear wants to rest a while.

Six bears hopping on one foot;
One of them will just stay put.

Five bears riding on a horse;
One of them falls off, of course.

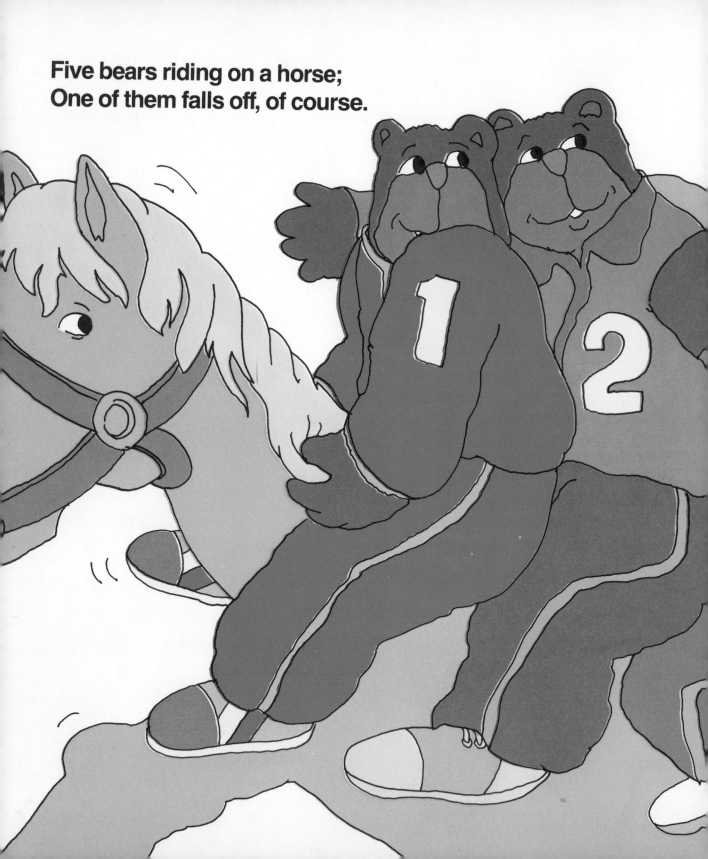

**Four bears left now, playing tag;
One bear finds a sleeping bag.**

Three bears sliding down the slope;
One gets tangled in a rope.

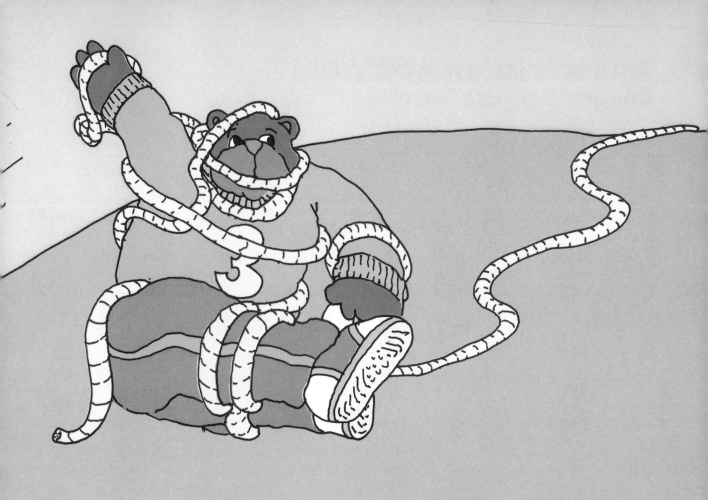

Two bears jogging huff, huff, puff;
One bear says he's had enough.

The last bear left is number one;
He's going home now,
That leaves none.